How to Make your Dog COME Without Being a BUTT-HEAD

Mike Deathe CPDT-KA

Published by FastPencil

Copyright © 2014 Mike Deathe, CPDT-KA

Published by FastPencil
307 Orchard City Drive
Suite 210
Campbell CA 95008 USA
info@fastpencil.com
(408) 540-7571
(408) 540-7572 (Fax)
http://www.fastpencil.com

While dog training itself is a rewarding and happy endeavor, any issues involving aggression should not be attempted without the supervision and direction of a professional trainer.

No part of this publication may be reproduced, stored in a retrieval system, or transmitted, in any form, or by any means, electronic, mechanical, photocopying, recording, or otherwise, without the prior consent of the publisher.

The Publisher makes no representations or warranties with respect to the accuracy or completeness of the contents of this book and specifically disclaim any implied warranties of merchantability or fitness for a particular purpose. Neither the publisher nor author shall be liable for any loss of profit or any commercial damages.

Printed in the United States of America.

First Edition

To my clients and my family …
Not to mention all the dogs who never came back!

Acknowledgments

To Every client who has graced me with the trust to train them and their dogs ...

Contents

Chapter 1	Who am I, calling you a butt-head?	1
Chapter 2	Just what is recall? And why is it so hard to learn?	3
Chapter 3	Wait! There are rules!	7
Chapter 4	Distraction	11
Chapter 5	Let the games begin!	13
Chapter 6	The backyard	17
Chapter 7	Freedom ... with strings attached	21
Chapter 8	Taking it to the streets	25
Chapter 9	What about the dog park?	27
Chapter 10	Long distance and emergency recall	31
Chapter 11	Frequency and consistency	35
	Conclusion	37

1
Who am I, calling you a butt-head?

Okay, please don't misunderstand me. I am not trying to insult you with the title of this book. Rather, I want to get your attention. The goal of teaching you how to get you pooch to come back to you when you call them is secondary. My primary goal is to get you to think about dog training in a different way!

In many ways, I train dogs the way most of us want to teach children. That being said, I for some reason have way more patience with my dogs than my own kids — just ask my sons and they will confirm. I think it has something to do with the fact my sons talk back and my dogs don't but that is just one man's opinion ...

With this book, I hope to give you a new way to look at your dog, as well as a very successful set of techniques that will have your dog coming when called on a regular and consistent basis.

So let's begin. My name is Mike Deathe and I will be your tour guide on this trip to understanding the why, what, how and where of teaching Fido to come to you when you call him! I started training dogs in 2008 purely by accident and have been blessed to make it a career. It was a trip though middle management, marriage, kids, career change, divorce and little bit of everything else that got me to here, but here are some things that might interest you…

- Certified Dog Trainer, CPDT-KA
- Canine Good Citizen Evaluator
- Written three other books on dog training (all on Amazon)
- Public speaker on dog training, as well as business coaching
- Occasional radio host
- Blogger
- Writer for several magazines
- Dad
- Friend
- All-around goof

So now you know a little bit about me and what this book is all about, i'll try to teach you — yes you, not the dog — about dogs & coming when called. It's a new take on an old problem, techniques that have worked for many people over the years. So quit thinking, turn the page and let's get down to the real question: just what the heck is recall anyway?

Mike Deathe, CPDT-KA

2
JUST WHAT IS RECALL? AND WHY IS IT SO HARD TO LEARN?

No surprise here. *Come when called,* or "recall" as some dog trainers like to call it, is just what is sounds like. You call Fido and he either comes to you or he does not — probably the latter, since you're reading this book. Not much more complicated than that! But the ways we teach, understand and react to recall will have a huge impact on our success. So let's start with why it is so hard to teach our dogs to do come when called reliably.

The short answer? **Recall always ends the fun for the dog.** Think about it:

❃ Stop sniffing that patch of grass and come here!
❃ Quit playing with your friends and come here!
❃ Don't you sniff that butt, you come here!
❃ Oh you did not just chase that squirrel! Come here right now!
❃ Just what do you think you are doing? Come right over here!

Are you starting understand why your dog thinks this "recall" command is a real downer? Let's face it: from your dog's perspective, this game sucks! I don't want to make light of coming when called, but instead I want to give you a different perspective on the situation.

These examples are also right out of the old "Alpha/Dominance" Playbook: you will do as I say because I am the human and you are the dog! Once again, it's not necessarily what your pooch would consider a good time or something he looks forward to doing. That we think the dog should come 100% of the time just because we are human proves just how far we need to come in training our dogs.

Let's just try a different path. Ask yourself these questions:

❊ Do your children say please or thank you 100% of the time?
❊ Do your children tell the truth 100% of the time?
❊ Do your children listen 100% of the time?
❊ Do your children do as they are asked 100% of the time?

Even if you don't have kids, think in general about the kids you know. What's your answer?

Unless you are completely full of *%!@, you're well aware the answer to these questions is *no*. The only way to fix these issues is to teach children to do these things. We know as parents that we must remind, reward, coach and even punish on occasion.

Tip #1

Punishment by definition is simply something that decreases the frequency of a behavior. Punishment does not mean or encourage being a butt-head (see the subtitle of the book). While I do think punishment is a part of learning, I just do not choose to use the word to mean physical or harsh

corrections. Sorry, the word punishment is not a bad word — only one that is misused on a regular basis. Now, back to the book!

How many times did you have to ask for a "please and thank you" from your kids in a restaurant? How many discussions did you have about lying, or paying attention? Trust me, many parents reading this book are still having these conversations!

Experts peg the intelligence level of the adult dog as that of a two or three year old toddler — and so physical corrections are just not going to work as well as some of our other options. Let's face it: some of you are not going to like my ideas and will think I am just dead wrong. But please just keep reading and try the ideas we are about to explore. If nothing else, I promise your training sessions will less confrontational and more fun!

Well, if the traditional way of teaching recall is to end the fun, then the logical way to proceed is to create more fun, right? So we'll use games to teach recall. It is really just that simple. But before we can play a game, we have to know the rules first. That's where we're headed in the next chapter …

3
Wait! There are rules!

Okay, so if you're going to play the games that teach recall, you'd better know the rules of the game. The rules are simple and easy to understand — but trust me, at times the difficulty will be remembering the rules and not allowing your frustration to take you down a different path.

Just implementing these simple ideas will improve your ability to get your dog to come when called! So here they are:

- **Never use frustration, anger or punishment when calling your dog.** If you are upset or angry, you will just have to fake it. Likewise, you are never allowed to call Fido to you and then punish him. Falling prey to either of these mistakes will only hurt the bond with your dog, as well as create confusion for the dog. Fido is left wondering whether he should expect Dr. Jekyll or Mr. Hide when he's called. Lets face it, would you come running to someone who was pissed off?

- **Lower your body position when attempting recall.** Once again, look at it from the dog's point of view. Humans, in most cases, are at least three times taller than dogs. How would you feel having an 18 or 19 foot tall giant calling you? Suffice it to say, dropping to your knee and avoiding direct eye contact (another threatening posture) will go a long way in getting your dog to come to you.

❋ **Use an uplifting and excited tone of voice when doing recall.** Almost everyone I know has seen *The Wizard of Oz* … and we all remember Glenda the Good Witch. You need to channel her voice when calling your dog. This is going to sound silly, but I'm serious, the goofier, happier and squeakier your voice, the better the results will be. Hint, hint: if you're not having fun, do you really think your dog is?

❋ **Be very aware of your body position when using recall.** If, for example, you move towards a dog while calling them, you will inadvertently trigger the oldest game in a dog's arsenal: chase. Fido will run from you, hoping you will chase him! This, after all, is a really fun game! However, if you take several steps back (away from the dog) while using recall, the dog will be enticed to chase after you … and that is what you are trying to get anyway!

❋ **Changing your behavior will, in the end, change your pooch's behaviors.** When this chase game behavior first happens, we think it's cute. But then we end up late for work and frustrated when the dog still wants to play the game. That's when our body language and our tone changes from cute to "I am getting angry." At that point, your dog's motivation for not coming changes. He still won't come when called, but now he does it out of fear because of your actions. Either way, the dog still doesn't come, but remembering this will help you stay positive.

❉ **There must be a reward 100% of the time when you are calling your dog.** The dog must understand that whatever distraction is keeping them from coming to you is less important than the reward they receive from Mom or Dad each time. The reward does not necessarily have to be food. It can be a favorite toy, a loving touch or even soft words of encouragement for a job well done. Nonetheless, a reward must follow every successful recall.

❉ **If you are going to use a hand signal with recall, *Keep it Simple*!** I simply take my arm and hold it straight out, and drop it straight down slapping the side of my leg. I mainly use the hand signal outdoors or in long distance recalls. Do not get too complicated with the words; my cue for recall is simply my dog's name. Whether you use the word *come* is totally up to you. Remember, words are for us, not the dogs. They don't speak English, so as far as I am concerned you can say "pineapple sherbet." Just don't overthink it.

Okay, so now you have the rules down and you are ready to move on to the games ... The next chapter does cover the games, including Ping Pong and Hide & Seek, but we must also discuss how the word **DISTRACTION** is going to shape how we teach and use these games. Otherwise, we are going to end up with dogs who come to us in the house but fall apart the minute they walk or run out the front door!

4
Distraction

Before we get to any games, let me explain what I mean by distraction. The idea of distraction acutally translates to any problem behavior we encounter with our dog. In this case, we'll deal specifically with distraction related to recall. Simply put, the more distracting or novel an environment, the harder a dog will have to work in that enviornment.

Is it harder to recall your dog in the front yard than it is inside your house? The answer should be a resounding yes. Why? Fewer distractions.

As you begin your training, you must start in the least distracting environment. And only as you improve, you must increase the difficulty of each level. Good news: the more areas and places you practice, the better your recall will be. Bad news: no matter what, you will never have 100% recall with your dog! The goal is reliable recall, and that will takes months of practice. Not days and certainly not hours ... so you had better be ready to practice!

The secret is simple: don't expect great recall in an environment where you have not practiced substantially. This, my friends, is the crux of the distraction problem — the problem I see daily as a dog trainer. Human beings do not put in the adequate time or effort in most cases to teach their dogs! So if you are smart, the games we'll cover will be taught and practiced not only inside the four walls of your home, but in every other enviornment where you want the technique to work.

Now that you understand distraction, let's move to the next step: the games of **Ping Pong** and **Hide and Seek.**

5
Let the games begin!

The first game we are going to play is **Ping Pong**. This game is very reminiscent to "monkey in the middle," and requires two people and the dog. The dog will be in the middle. Pick an area of your house with plenty of room. A hallway or living room works great! Have each person start with three to five treats. Stand at opposite ends of the room and take turns calling the dog back and forth until the treats are gone. The cue or command here? Simply call the dog's name. I usually don't even use the word come …

To me, "come" is redundant, and just one more spoken word your dog has to master. Just build the understanding that when you call a dog's name, he should check in. This game does two things. First, it teaches Fido that every time he recalls to his name, he gets a reward (the treat). Secondly, Fido learns that when he can see you and hears you use his name, he needs to come to you and check in.

The only other rule I insist on: the dog must sit and allow you to grab his or her collar before receiving the treat and getting released to the other person for the next recall. Why? Simple. Many dog bite cases result from a person grabbing a collar and the dog redirecting back with a bite. So if we include asking for a sit and a collar grab into every recall, and we reward the dog for this behavior, our dog ends up liking his collar grabbed and understands that part of recall is being restrained, not running off to start a game of chase.

Now don't forget — once you have the game down in one area of the house, move to the next. Practice in every area you want recall to work so that includes hall ways, up and down stairs and all the different rooms in the house. If we make distraction our friend, then before too long, recall will be our friend as well.

The second game we are going to play is **Hide and Seek,** and yes it is basically the same game you played as a kid. The major difference is that this game adds a new element. The dog must learn that if he can hear you, whether or not he can see you, he must find you to get that reward. In the end, what we want are dogs who understand that coming to us is the name of the game, as well as the fastest way to a rewarding experience. So the end goal should still be the same with either game: dog who comes when called, sits, allows us to grab that collar and waits patiently to be released back.

So how does Hide and Seek work? Well, you start by having several treat jars placed all over the house. I have eight located around my house! You can put them in bathrooms, laundry rooms, the kitchen and even bedrooms. Having the treat jars all over the place simply helps remind you to play the game. See a jar? Time to practice! For example, I keep one jar in the laundry room and when I am doing a load of laundry I call one of my dogs to me, and if the dog shows up, I ask for a sit, grab the collar and offer a treat. If I am upstairs in the bathroom brushing my teeth, I call a dog and follow that process. Before too long, your dog realizes that whether you're in sight or not, she needs to find you. Why, you ask? Because we are making it fun and rewarding to play the game!

To add a twist, you can incorporate another person into the game. Have one person hold the dog while the other hides somewhere in the house with a **Jackpot** (two or three treats) in hand, then calls the dog. When the dog eventually finds you, she gets all the Jackpot of treats at once! Adults don't really get into this game, but if there are kids in the family, this is one of the best times involve them. My youngest son would actually make his bed so he could pretend to be a pillow under the covers, tricking the dog. What an unexpected benefit of dog training ... a six-year-old who makes his bed, not to mention the ability to include kids in the training process!

I recommend practicing these games several times each day and keeping the training session short, no more than 10 minutes each. As with all training, it is not the amount of training, it is the consistency in which you train. So it is better to have one good, short, positive session every day for a month instead of 10 really long sessions that your dog tunes out after 10-15 minutes. As I said earlier, start small (distraction wise) and build from there. Once we achieve good success inside the house, let's up the ante and the distraction ... to the backyard!

6

THE BACKYARD

So you are feeling pretty good about your progress. Ping Pong and Hide and Seek are going great and you have been practicing hard! Then, one day, your wonderful little pooch sneaks out the front door and takes off for the hills completely and totally ignores you. At this point, you start doubting all your hard work and wondering if you are ever gonna get this damn dog to come when called!? You might even at this point wonder if the guy who wrote this book is a crackpot.

Remember, though, that distraction is our toughest nut to crack. And all we have done so far is practice inside your house. So let's be smart: now is not the time to give up, but rather the time to take our games outside! Now we want to upgrade the distraction, but we don't want so much distraction that the dog fails … so enter the backyard!

If you think about it, the backyard is the next logical step. We can play Ping Pong and we can also play Hide and Seek right there in the backyard. In fact, Ping Pong becomes a little easier in the backyard because you can play by yourself. Just ignore the dog for a period of time and then wait for her to wander away, just so I can call her back. You're reinforcing the dog getting a reward every time she comes back.

Likewise, Hide and Seek becomes a little bit easier in the backyard, even if you might feel a little foolish while you're doing it. After all, you will be hiding behind the air conditioner, behind a tree, behind a bush ... using anything you can in the backyard to visually separate yourself from the dog. If there are kids in the family, you can still use them just like you did in the house to help you along with the training, but the real goal in the backyard is simply to upgrade the distraction level. Fido is learning one step at a time that it is more rewarding to pay attention and check in with his owner than it is to ignore.

So now you find yourself once again feeling a little bit cocky. Things are going great and you want to take this to the next level. So just how will you do it? Well, the first step is a trip to the pet store to buy what we trainers call a long line! Let me be clear, this is not a retractable leash in fact I'll be honest, if there was one thing I could outlaw in dog training it would be the retractable leash! See my rant ...

All I want you to purchase is a very long leash. Depending on the size your dog it could be anywhere from 15 to 25 feet. What on God's green earth are you going to use this for? Simple: you'll teach your dog recall in the front yard. That's right, you are heading to the front yard to practice ... the one spot you know your dog won't come back!

A dog trainer's rant ...

Don't get me wrong. For certain dogs, those who have already been taught to walk nicely on a leash, retractable leashes would be fine. But from what I have seen, most folks who buy them do not fit into that category. Instead, they are folks whose dogs have had little if any training and now have the freedom to not only torment their owners but now also have the freedom to torment others as well.

The other aspect of these leashes that drive me nuts is that they encourage pulling. Let me break it down for you. Your dog doesn't know how or what a leash is for, either because he's a puppy or has never been taught. And you put him on this retractable leash. You try to be a good dog owner and not give too much freedom and you keep him close. However, he is pulling just like he always does and bang! The mistake. You accidentally pull that little trigger and Fido all of the sudden gets more leash. Trust me, it only takes one time for Fido to figure out the best way to get more leash is to simply keep pulling.

One other thing you might want to consider before going with one of these leashes is the sheer number of folks who have had their fingers amputated or severely injured while using them! Just Google "finger amputation with retractable leashes." Or better yet, take a look at the packaging of one of these leashes. They all now have this particular warning, I would imagine, to keep from getting sued …

Okay. Back to the long line and the front yard …

7

Freedom ... with Strings Attached

All right, we are feeling pretty good about ourselves. Recall is working well in the house and we've even started practicing in the backyard! Things are going great ... except for the damn front yard.

We all know this is one of the toughest areas to recall your pooch. Why? The front yard your dog's garden of Eden. It's the forbidden fruit, the area where your dog is never allowed to be off the leash. So when Fido finds himself off leash, he runs for the hills. The fact is, the front yard is an environment that most dogs rarely get the chance to work in, therefore a distraction they have never experienced!

Let me put this a different way ... If you were told this morning that you had to take an entire class of second graders to an amusement park, would you be excited about the idea? Of course you wouldn't! You would probably be terrified realizing that you would spend the entire day chasing second graders and trying to get them to listen to you. However, if you took those same second graders to the amusement park for 30 straight days, by day 30 they would be listening better, behaving better and actually paying attention to you. Why? The shine had been taken off the amusement park and the environment would be less distracting.

The problem is that as dog owners we don't have nearly the same patience that we do with kids. The long line is simply the way that we will get Fido to think he has some freedom and allow us the time needed to take the shine off of the front yard. This is the point where we start attaching some strings to keep Fido safe and keep us in control of the training.

To start practicing in the front yard, the string we attach is the long line. A long line is simply a long leash. For small dogs, 10 to 15 feet is plenty long enough. For a large dog, you might go as long as 25 or 30 feet. Any big-box pet retail store will have these longer leashes.

So let's get to it ... You have your dog, you have your long line, you're in the front yard and of course you better have treats in your pocket! The rest of this technique is pretty simple. Start walking, allow your dog to go sniff, investigate and experience this entire front yard area!

The only rule is simple: when the dog reaches the end of your long line, stop, call your dog back to you, ask for a sit, grab the collar, give the treat. Then comes the magic: release the dog back to checking his "pee mail" or getting his "sniff on"! Each time the dog reaches the end of the long line, call him back and reward and repeat!

The dog feels she has freedom because she can get further and further away from you. And you are building trust, only calling the dog back when we reach the end of the line! Add the fact that we give a treat when the dog comes back and then even allow the dog to go back to what they were doing. Pretty soon, the dog realizes the golden rule of recall. **Recall doesn't actually end the fun,** your dog will realize. **Really, it's just a simple check-in in with my owner! After all, once I check in I get to go back to doing what I want.**

The cool part about this technique is that, over time, your dog will learn that he has a halo approximately the same size as the long line you have been practicing with. You will have a dog who understands the benefit of continually checking in with his owner! And after all, isn't that what we really want? Now keep in mind, practice at this point is in your front yard area or your block only. The goal here is not perfection, rather only to get Fido used to this small amount of freedom so the front yard becomes an easier area to work in or around. The next chapters will get us even further out there in the nasty world of distractions. But for now ask yourself this: how do you eat an elephant? Simple, one bite at a time! So lets get to eating …

8

Taking it to the Streets

Okay, this chapter is going to be short and sweet — but very important! As I said earlier, you eat an elephant one bite at a time. We've already started this book with the understanding that we work in the house, we get good in the house, we work in the backyard, we get good in the backyard, we work in the front yard with a long line, we get good in the front yard, we expand to the houses around our block. If we have done our jobs correctly, we have a dog at this point who's pretty good at recall but is still going to be distractible in unfamiliar areas.

So our next step is simple: more of the same, just in a different place. Keep expanding the area that you're walking in with the long line. Now a word of caution here: using a long line to walk your dog in a neighborhood has both good qualities and bad qualities. If you live on a very busy street, using a long line to walk your dog is going to be problematic at best. Likewise, you are not going to want to walk your dog on a 25 to 30 foot long line during periods of the day when there will be 15 other dogs walking at the same time in an area. It is up to you to make good decisions and keep Fido in situations that increase his learning curve, not destroy it!

If there is one overriding rule to dog training, it is Keep it Simple Stupid. Success builds success — and failure builds failure. This is exactly the reason why we take levels of distraction from the least to the most. If you become impatient pushing your dog too far too fast or put her in situations she cannot handle, you will simply become frustrated and your dog will not learn. It is just this frustration that probably led you to buy this book. And it is also this type of frustration that fills our animal shelters on a daily, weekly, monthly and yearly basis!

So as you move from your front yard to your block and then on to the neighborhood, do it in a manner in which both you and Fido can handle the increases in distraction. Constantly be thinking of what your dog can handle how you can improve it. There is still one more area in which you can practice and we are going to discuss that area in the next chapter. However, this area can be both a great idea and a really bad idea depending on how responsible you and those around you are with their dogs. With that being said, let's move on to the next chapter and talk about dog parks!

9

What about the dog park?

All right, so here we are. By this point, we have a dog who is reasonably reliable at recall. We have a dog who understands that checking in with his owner gets him rewards. We have a dog who also understands that recall is not necessarily a bad thing, a dog who has practiced in increasing levels of distraction. Many of you will simply stop here and be satisfied with what you have and I'm cool with that.

However, there is still one kind of recall you have not dealt with. You have not taught your dog to recall over long distances or deal with ultra high-end distractions. Many trainers will call this emergency recall training. Some, in fact, will even use a special emergency word to train their dog. I do it a little bit differently. Instead of a word we are going to simply use a whistle (those of you who can whistle really loud are in luck). For others like me, who can't whistle to save their lives, you will simply need to look for a coach's whistle or even a clicker that has a whistle built into it. They are available online just search for them… But before we get to the how-to on this technique we need to discuss the area in which I usually train this technique in… The dog park!

Let's face it: what is the most distracting environment you can put your dog in? Well, in my humble opinion, it is the dog park. Think about it just like the example I used earlier of second graders and an amusement park. A dog park is just that to your pooch. So, with training, if you can get your dog to recall at the dog park with all of his friends present and all the distractions around, you, my friend, have a good recall dog. The dog park also gives us a big area of space, which is really awesome when you're trying to teach long distance recalls!

BUT dog parks have changed so much over the last three to five years …

So before I talk to you about how to use a dog park and how to teach emergency recall and/or long distance recall, I want to go on a brief rant about dog parks. You, as the owner of a dog, have the responsibility to be that dog's advocate!

If you have a dog that does not do well around other dogs, then you should not be at a dog park. If you have a dog who is fearful, you have a dog that does not belong in a dog park. If you are the type of person who cannot focus long enough to pay attention to your own dog at the dog park, neither of you should be there. If you know your dog has aggressive tendencies, you should not be at a dog park.

The problem is, each and every time I go to a dog park now, I see dogs with some (if not all) of these issues, mixed in with the great dog owners and parents who have always enjoyed utilized and taken advantage of dog parks. So while I'm going to teach you about the techniques I've used at dog parks, I need to make it clear: only work in a dog park if you feel comfortable.

When I am deciding whether or not to go into a dog park, my technique is simple: I usually will walk my dog through the dog park on a leash on the outside edges of the park until I have covered the entire park. I've seen not only all the owners, but their dogs from a distance. Then and only then will I make the decision whether I want to take my dog off leash. You would be amazed how many times my dog and I have simply walked around the park only to see a couple of hooligan dogs or bleepity bleep owners and then walked directly back to the car to leave.

My goal here is not to bash on dog parks. I think they serve a wonderful purpose. However, just like everything else in our society and our world today, it only takes a few rotten apples to ruin the bushel for everyone. So be warned, this last technique I want to teach you about recall is totally up to you. Be an advocate for your dog and don't ever put your dog in a situation that could ruin all the hard work that you have put in until now.

10

LONG DISTANCE AND EMERGENCY RECALL

After reading the last chapter, you and Fido have decided you're ready to work on long distance and emergency recall. You're at the dog park, you've checked out all the areas, seen all the dogs and now you feel totally comfortable that this is a good learning environment for you and Fido. So what's next?

First we need to learn a little bit about what dog trainers call combining cues. By this I mean having two separate commands or cues that mean the same thing. We are going to make both a whistle and calling the dog by name mean the same thing — and bring the same response from Fido.

First off, why would we even want to do that? Simple: I want you to be able to use the whistle for our emergency recall. Let's say your dog sees a distraction, another dog, while you are trying to get him to come to you. Chances are pretty good that Fido just might ignore you! Now don't take this wrong, but with his decision, Fido is trying to tell you that sniffing another dog's butt is way more rewarding than simply coming to you and getting a cookie. We need to have a way to interrupt Fido's brain, if only for a split second, so we can reconnect with him and remind him that coming to us is the correct choice.

This, my friends, is where the whistle comes in. By simply blowing a loud sharp whistle, we can interrupt Fido's thinking process long enough for him to look at us and in most cases convince him that coming to you is more rewarding than checking out the other dog. But without that interruption and thought process, you stand a very slim chance of success.

Some of you are asking, *What do you mean a chance! I want perfect recall, I want my dog to come back to me 100% of the time.* Well, folks, I am what's called a realist and trust me whether you are dealing with dogs, children, spouses, cats or sea monkeys, there is no such thing in this world as 100%. There will always be that unexpected distraction, something more interesting or rewarding, or in many cases no consistency or frequency with our practice that will in the end get us the results we do not want. That being said, I have found the best way to make my dog more reliable in recall is simply to practice and to be ready for the unexpected.

The other side to this technique is getting the two different cues to mean the same thing — in this case using the dog's name and blowing the whistle both meaning come here. Now by this point in training, your dog already understands that when she hears her name, she should come to her owner, sit, wait for the collar to be grabbed and get that paycheck (a cookie, a kind word or even a soft touch)! All we have to do is figure out how to combine the whistle into this equation.

It's really basic learning theory and very simple. The unknown cue must come first... While we are practicing, we blow the whistle first, wait several seconds then call the dog, wait for the dog to recall and then back to the basics you already know: sit, collar grab, reward. The more we practice, the more the commands meld together meaning the same thing.

You have most likely already done this with your dog with hand signals and the words for commands like sit and down but just never realized it. If we did it in reverse, called the dog then blew the whistle, it would not work because the dog would simply ignore the whistle because he already knew what the first command meant. In essence, the whistle would become background noise with no meaning.

So once you really break it down and understand how to teach your emergency/whistle recall, it becomes pretty obvious why you would use it in an emergency situation. The whistle simply becomes a way to break a dog's fixation on some external distraction so that you stand a better chance of getting your dog to come to you. Obviously, like anything else you've read in this book, the more you practice the better it will get and the more you can expect out of your dog, and obviously practicing at the dog park will be full of distractions and distance!

11

Frequency and consistency

Okay so we pretty much covered everything about recall that I want to teach you — except for two little words. I've hinted at them throughout the entire book: **FREQUENCY and CONSISTENCY!** To explain these two words, I'll tell you what I relay to every dog training client I work with: if you are not *frequently consistent* or *consistently frequent* with the things I teach you, you're going to end up being very disappointed in the results you get from working with me.

I guess, in a roundabout way, this has been my warranty statement since the day I started my business. It is why I don't like being called the dog trainer and would rather be known as a people trainer. Folks, it's not the dogs I have to train. It's you. And people very rarely tend to be consistent or frequent with anything — that includes me too. Let's face it, this is the reason why diets, working out, quitting smoking or any other resolution seems to be so damn hard!

I include this chapter as a reminder to have fair expectations of what your dog will and will not do. Animals are not computers, machines or things that can be controlled. Dogs are simply beings we want to share our lives with, so don't look to control the the dog you live with. Instead, learn to live with the dog you live with. In the end I think both of you will be happier for it.

Final note on the training you'll be doing: the word **fun** is very important in everyone's life, your dog's included. If the training you do is militant, controlling or hard, neither you or the dog will enjoy it. And ironically, neither of you will learn from it.

Think back to your own educational background. Did you learn more in the classes you enjoyed or did you learn more in the classes you hated? Don't forget to have fun! That's probably what you were looking for when you decided to bring a dog into your house. I wish you all the luck in the world, but know it has way more to do with consistency and frequency than luck!

CONCLUSION

Well you made it, folks, the end of the book! First, I want to say thanks for buying the book. And secondly, I really hope you got something here in these pages that will help you and your dog communicate better. The information in these pages has come from many years of helping folks with the come when called/recall problem. I promise if you put in the time, practice, and spend the time *with* your dog versus *against* your dog, really anything can be accomplished!

If you enjoyed the book, there's plenty more where this came from! We have several other books, as well as many videos on our YouTube channel. We have an active blog, Facebook and other social media outlets. You name it, we've done it — in an attempt to teach folks to speak Dog as a Second Language.

While writing these books has been a pleasure, my true passion is public speaking! I love spreading the word about positive, scientific-based dog training. Let's face it, there are many people out there who have no idea how easy it is to train a dog or how enjoyable it can be! So simply Google me, Mike Deathe, or visit our business page www.kissdogtraining.com [http://www.kiss-dogtraining.com] (and yes it does stand for Keep It Simple

Stupid) if you or your group would like to have me come to give a presentation!

A final thought, and a request if you don't mind ... as a small author, one of the greatest gifts you the reader can give me is a few minutes of your time and a review online of this book. This is information I am passionate about and I feel will help lots of people out there. I just need your help to get the word out! So with that being said, thank you for reading the book, thank you for buying the book and thank you for being a part of training your dog the Keep It Simple Stupid way!

Mike

FastPencil
http://www.fastpencil.com

www.ingramcontent.com/pod-product-compliance
Lightning Source LLC
Chambersburg PA
CBHW052044070526
44584CB00018B/2599